Edward Clodd

The Childhood of the World

A simple account of man in early times. Vol. 1

Edward Clodd

The Childhood of the World
A simple account of man in early times. Vol. 1

ISBN/EAN: 9783337370299

Printed in Europe, USA, Canada, Australia, Japan

Cover: Foto ©Andreas Hilbeck / pixelio.de

More available books at **www.hansebooks.com**

THE
CHILDHOOD OF THE WORLD;

A Simple Account

—OF—

MAN IN EARLY TIMES.

—BY—

EDWARD CLODD, F.R.A.S.

" *As a child that cries,*
But, crying, knows his father near."

IN MEMORIAM.

SECOND AMERICAN EDITION.

New York:
ASA K. BUTTS & CO., 36 DEY STREET.

1873.

PREFACE.

For the information of parents and others into whose hands this book may fall, it may be stated that it is an attempt, in the absence of any kindred elementary work, to narrate, in as simple language as the subject will permit, the story of man's progress from the unknown time of his early appearance upon the earth, to the period from which writers of history ordinarily begin.

That an acquaintance with the primitive condition of man should precede the study of any single department of his later history is obvious, but it must be remembered that such knowledge has become attainable only within the last few years, and at present enters but little, if at all, into the course of study at schools.

Thanks to the patient and careful researches of men of science, the way is rapidly becoming clearer for tracing the steps by which, at ever-varying rates of progress, different races have advanced from savagery to civilization, and for thus giving a completeness to the history of mankind which the assumptions of an arbitrary chronology would render impossible.

As the Table of Contents indicates, the First Part of this book describes the progress of man in material things, while the Second Part seeks to explain his mode of advance from lower to higher stages of religious belief.

Although this work is written for the young, I venture to hope that it will afford to older persons who will accept the simplicity of its style, interesting information concerning primitive man.

In thinking it undesirable to encumber the pages of a work of this class with foot-notes and references, I have been at some pains to verify the statements made, the larger body of which may be found in the works of Tylor, Lubbock, Nilsson, Waitz, and other ethnologists, to whom my obligations are cordially expressed.

I am fully conscious how slenderly each department of human progress has been dealt with in this work, but in seeking to compass a great subject within a small space, it has been my anxiety to break the continuity of the story as little as possible.

E. C.

133 Brecknock Road, London,
December, 1872.

CONTENTS.

PART II.

THE

CHILDHOOD OF THE WORLD.

PART I.

I. INTRODUCTORY.

EVERYTHING in this wide world has a history; that is, it has something to tell or something to be found out about what it was, and how it has come to be what it is.

Even of the small stones lying in the roadway, or about the garden, clever men have, after a great deal of pains-taking, found out a history more wonderful than all the fairy stories you have been told; and if this be true, as true it is, of dead stones and many other things which cannot speak, you may believe that a history stranger still can be written about some living things.

And it is the history of the most wonderful living thing that this world has ever seen that I want to tell you. You will perhaps think that I am about to describe to you some curly-haired, big-tusked, fierce-looking mon-

ster that lived on the earth thousands of years ago, for
children (and some grown-up people too) are apt to think
that things are wonderful only when they are big, which
is not true. To show you what I mean: the beautiful
six-sided wax cells which the bee makes are more curious
than the rough hut which the chimpanzee—an African
monkey—piles together; and the tiny ants that keep
plant-lice and milk them just as we keep cows to give us
milk, and that catch the young of other ants to make
slaves of them, are more wonderful than the huge and
dull rhinoceros.

Well, it is about *yourself* that I am going to talk, for
I want you to learn, as far as we are able to find out, how
it is that you are *what* you are, and *where* you are. Remember, I do not say *how* your are, or *why* you are, for
God alone knows that, and He has told the secret to no
one here, although, maybe, He will tell it us one day
elsewhere.

Perhaps you have thought that there is nothing very
wonderful in being where you are, or in possessing the
good things which you enjoy; that people have always had
them, or if not, that they had only to buy them at the
shops; and that from the first day man lived on the
earth he could cook his food, and have ices and dessert
after it; could dress himself well, write a good hand,
live in a fine house, and build splendid churches with
stained glass windows, just as he does now-a-days.

It you have thought so, you are wrong, and I wish to

set you right, and show you that man was once wild and rough and savage, frightened at his own shadow, and still more frightened at the roar of thunder and the quiver of lightning, which he thought were the clapping of the wings and the flashing of the eyes of the angry Spirit, as he came flying from the sun ; and that it has taken many thousands of years for man to become as wise and skillful as we now see him to be.

For just as you had to learn your A, B, C to enable you to read at all, and just as you are learning things day by day which will help you to be useful when you grow up and are called upon to do your share of work in this world, where all idleness is sin, so man had to begin learning, and to get at facts step by step along a toilsome road.

And instead of being told, as we are told, why a certain thing is done, and which is the best way to do it, he had to find out these things for himself by making use of the brains God had given him, and had often to do the same thing over and over again, as you have sometimes with a hard spelling lesson, before he was able to do it well.

Now there are several reasons for the belief that man was once wild and naked, and that only by slow degrees did he become clothed and civilized. For instance, there have been found in Europe, Asia, Africa, and America, but especially in Europe, thousands of tools and weapons which were shaped and used by men ages upon ages ago, and which are just like the tools and weapons used by savages living now-a-days in various parts of the earth, and among whom no traces of a civilized past can be found.

Far across the wind-tossed seas, far away in such places as Australia, Borneo, and Ceylon, islands which you must learn to find out on a map of the world, or on a globe, there live at this day creatures so wild that if you saw them you would scarcely believe that they were human beings and not wild animals in the shape of men, covering themselves with mud, feeding on roots, and living in wretched huts or in woods under the shelter of trees. The word "savage" means *one who lives in the woods.*

In telling you how the earliest men lived I shall want you to go back with me a great many years, even before the histories of different countries begin. For men had to learn a great deal before they were clever enough to *write* histories of themselves and live together as we English people do, making a nation; many, many centuries —and a century is a hundred years—passed away before they left any trace behind to tell us that they lived, other than the tools I am about to describe, or broken pottery and scratchings on bones.

Yes, I shall take you past not only the Conquest, but past the day when in this England—then called Britain— the wild people dwelt in mud huts, lived on fruits and the flesh of wild animals, stained their bodies with the blue

juice of the woad-plant, and worshiped trees and the
sun and moon, even to the day when no sea flowed between England and France, when there was no German
Ocean and no English Channel!

For you must take now on trust what by and by you
will be able to prove the truth of for yourself, when you
learn lessons from the rocks and hills themselves, instead
of from books about them, that this world is, like the other
worlds floating with it in the great star-filled spaces, very,
very old and ever-changing,—so old that men make all
sorts of guesses about its birthday; and that, unlike us
who become wrinkled and gray, this dear old world
keeps ever fresh and ever beautiful, brightened by the
smiling sunlight of God playing over its face.

Now, it would be making another guess—and, as we
shall never know whether we have guessed right, what is
the use of guessing?—to say how many years man has
lived here. It is enough for us to know—and this is no
guess—that the good Being who made the world put man
on it at the best and fittest time, and that He makes
nothing in vain, whether it be rock, tree, flower, fish,
bird, beast, or man.

But although God left man to find out very much for
himself, He gave him the tools wherewith to work.
Eyes wherewith to see, ears wherewith to hear, feet
wherewith to walk, hands wherewith to handle,—these
were given for the use of the man himself, by which I
mean the mind, soul, or spirit, which is man. Perhaps

we may best call it the thinking part, because the word
" man" comes from a very old word which means *to think*;
therefore a man is *one who thinks*.   When names were
given to things, some word was fixed upon which best described the thing.   " Brute" comes from a word meaning
raw or *rough*, and so man is distinguished from the brutes
which are in some things like him, and from the plants
and trees, which are like him in that they breathe, by
being known as the *thinking* being.

If I sometimes break off my story to explain the
meaning of certain words, you will one day learn to
thank me for it, because, as you have already seen, there
is a reason, and sometimes a very beautiful reason, for the
names which things bear; and it is not less strange than
true, that words often tell us more of the manners and
doings of people who, silent now, used to speak them,
than we can find out from the remains they have left behind them.

In one case, the words they used to speak are the only
clue we have to the fact that a people who were our forefathers once lived in Asia.   They have left no traces (so
far as we can find out) of the tools which they used, of
the houses they lived in, or of writings on rocks or bricks,
and yet we know that they must have been, because the
words they spoke have come down to us, and are really
used by us in different forms and with different meanings,
of which I will give you a proof.

You know that the girls in a family are called the

"daughters." That word comes from a word very much like it, by which these people of old,—the Aryans, as we have named them—called their girls, and which means a *milking-maid.* Now, we know by this that they had got beyond the savage state, and that they must have kept goats and cows for the milk which they gave. Thus much a simple word tells us. In the same way, if the English people had died off the face of the earth, and left no records behind them other than remains of the words they uttered, we should know that English girls had learned to *spin*, because in course of time unmarried women were called *spinsters.*

II. MAN'S FIRST WANTS.

I have now to tell you that the first men were placed here wild and naked, knowing nothing of the great riches stored up in the earth beneath them, and only after a long time making it yellow with the waving corn, and digging out of it the iron and other metals so useful to mankind.

The first thought of man was about the wants of his body; his first desire was to get food to eat, fire for warmth, and some place for shelter when night came on, and wild beasts howled and roared around him.

See how, in the first step he had to take, man is unlike the brutes.

Wherever God has placed the brute, He has given it the covering best fitted for the place in which it lives,

and has supplied its proper food close at hand. But
God has placed man here naked, and left him to seek for
himself the food and clothing best suited to that part of
the world in which he lives. If God had given man
thick, hair-covered skin he could not have moved from
place to place with comfort, and so man is made naked,
but given the power of reasoning about things, and act-
ing by reason. The brute remains the brute he always
was, while man never stops, but improves upon what
those who lived before him have done.

Man has not the piercing eye of the eagle, but he has
the power of making instruments which not only bring
into view stars whose light has taken a thousand years
to reach the earth, but which also tell us what metals are
in the sun and other stars; man has not the swiftness
of the deer, but he has the power of making steam-en-
gines to carry him sixty miles in an hour; man has not
the strength of the horse, but he has put machines together which can do the work of a hundred horses.

Whatever power man has, whether of body or of mind,
improves by use. The savage, who has to make con-
stant use of his bodily powers to secure food, is by practice, fleeter of foot and quicker of sight than civilized
man who, using the power of his mind, excels the savage
in getting knowledge and making good and also bad use
of it.

I have said that the first things man wanted were food,
warmth, and shelter.

Ages before he lived here, the streams of fresh water had run down the mountain sides and through the valleys they had helped to make, and they were running still, never resting, so that man had little trouble in quenching his thirst, and would of course keep near the stream. But the food he needed was not to be had so easily. The first things he fed on would be wild fruits and berries, and the first place he lived in would be under some tree or over-hanging rock or in some cave. He might wish to eat of the fish that glided past him in the river, and of the reindeer that bounded past him into the depths of the forest; but these were not to be had without weapons to slay them.

There are few things which the wonderfully made hand of man cannot do, but it must have tools to work with. A man cannot cut wood or meat without a knife, he cannot write without a pen, or drive in nails without a hammer.

III. MAN'S FIRST TOOLS.

One of the first things which man needed was therefore some sharp-edged tool, which must of course be harder than the thing he wanted to cut. He knew nothing of the metals, although some of them, not the hardest, lay near the surface, and he therefore made use of the stones lying about. Men of science (that is, men *who know*, because "science" comes from a word meaning *to know*) have given the name "Age of Stone" to that far-off time when stone and such things as bone, wood, and horn, were made into various kinds of tools. Flints were very much used, because, by a hard blow, flakes like the blade of a knife could be broken off them. Other flints were shaped to a point, or into rough sorts of hammers, by chipping with a rounded pebble, or other stone. Many of them are in form like an almond, having a cutting edge all round. Their sizes differ, some being six inches long and three inches wide, while others are rather larger.

These oldest stone weapons, unsharpened by grinding and unpolished, have been chiefly found in places known as the "drift;" that is, buried underneath the gravel, and clay, and stones which have been *drifted* or carried down by the rivers in their ceaseless flow.

In these early days of man's history huge wild animals shared Europe with him. There were mammoths, or woolly-haired elephants, rhinoceroses, hippopotamuses; there were cave-lions, cave-bears, cave-hyænas, and other beasts of a much larger size than are found in the world at this day.

That they lived at the same time that man did is certain, because under layers of earth their bones have been found side by side with his, and with the weapons which he made.

Year after year man learnt to shape his tools and weapons better, until really well-formed spear-heads, daggers, hatchets, hammers, and other implements were made, and at a far later date he had learnt the art of polishing them. Remember that first in what is called the "old Stone Age" men learnt to chip stones, and afterwards, in what is called the "Newer Stone Age," to grind and polish them.

The better-shaped tools and weapons have been chiefly found in caves, which, as books about the earth will tell you, were hollowed out by water ages before any living thing dwelt here. These caves were used by men not only to live in, but also to bury their dead in; and from the different remains found in and near them, it is thought that feasts were held when the burials took place, and that food and weapons were put with the dead because their friends thought that such things were needed by them as they traveled the long journey to another world. I should tell you that but very few bones of primitive man have been found, and this is not to be wondered at when we remember how much more lasting is the work of man than are his remains, and also that from an early period the burning of dead bodies was common.

The great help to man of the weapons I have described to you against the attacks of the wild animals is easily understood, for with them he was able not only to defend himself and his family, but to kill the huge creatures, and thus get food for the mouths that were always increasing in number. That he did kill and eat them, -

and clothe himself in their skins and make their jaw-bones into strong weapons, is certain.

It is surprising to think how many things the first men had to do with the stones they roughly shaped. They cut down trees, and perhaps by the aid of fire scooped them out to make canoes, for it was plain to them that wood floated on the water; they killed their food, cut it up, broke the bones to suck out the marrow; cracked sea-shells to get out the fish inside them, besides doing many other things with what would seem to us blunt and clumsy tools.

While we are talking about this Stone Age I should tell you that there are found in different parts of the world stone ruins of very great age and various sizes, some built of stone pillars covered with a flat stone for roof, others built to a point like the great pyramids of Egypt.

These, like the caves, were used to bury the dead in, but sometimes were built to mark the place where some great deed was done, or where something very wonderful had happened. The piling together of stones was an easy and lasting way of keeping such things fresh in men's minds, just as we erect statues in honor of our great men, or build something in memory of their acts of bravery, nobleness, or love. When built as tombs for the dead, their size depended upon the rank of the person to be laid within them. The circles of standing stones—like that at Stonehenge—are thought to have been built for worship of some kind.

You have learnt, then, that during the time when weapons and tools of stone were made men lived a wild, roaming life, eating roots, berries, and fruits, and, in a raw state, the flesh of such animals as they killed, and, sad to say, some of them eating the flesh of their fellow-man ; clothing themselves, little or much as they needed, in the skins of animals, which they sewed together with bone needles, using the sinews for thread ; and now we have to speak about the first mode of getting a fire.

IV. FIRE.

There are a great many curious stories which profess to give an account of the way in which fire was first obtained, but they are a part of that guess-work about things which is ever going on, and which brings us no nearer the truth. Men have ever been quick to make use of what we call their " wits " (which word comes from an old word used by our forefathers, meaning *understanding*) or their common sense, and common sense taught them that fire was to be had by rubbing two pieces of wood together. In making their flint weapons sparks would fly, but they saw that the flints themselves could not be set on fire. When they felt cold they rubbed their hands together and warmth came to them. They tried what could be done by running a blunt pointed stick along a groove of its own making in another piece of wood, and they found first that each got heated, then that sparks flew, then that flame burst out.

Travelers tell us that savages can produce fire in a few seconds in this way, and that in the northern seas of Europe the islanders find a bird so fat and greasy that all they have to do is to draw a wick through its body, and on lighting it the bird burns away as a candle does.

And fire was as useful in the days I am writing about as travelers find it now in giving protection from the wild beasts at night, so that man had many reasons for keeping his fire always burning by heaping on it the wood which was ready to his hand in such abundance.

V. COOKING AND POTTERY.

At first men ate flesh raw, as some northern tribes do now, but afterwards they would learn to cook it, and this they did by simply putting the meat direct to the fire. Afterwards they would dig a hole and line it with the hard hide of the slain animal, fill it with water, put the meat in, and then make stones red-hot, dropping them in until the water was hot enough and the meat cooked. Then a still better way would be found out of boiling the food in vessels set over the fire, which were daubed outside with clay to prevent their being burnt. Thus men learnt—seeing how hard fire made the clay—to use it by itself and to shape it into rough pots, which were dried either in the sun or before the fire, and hence arose the beautiful art of making earthenware.

VI. DWELLINGS.

Besides living in caves, holes were dug in the ground, a wall being made of the earth which was thrown out, and a covering of tree-boughs put over it. Sometimes where blocks of stone were found lying loosely, they were placed together, and a rude, strong kind of hut made in this way.

There have been found in lakes, especially in Swiss lakes, remains of houses which were built upon piles driven into the bed of the lake. The shape of many of these piles shows that they were cut with stone hatchets. and this proves that people lived in this curious fashion in very early times. It is thought that they did so to be freer from the attacks of their enemies and of wild beasts.

These lake dwellers, as they are called (and they not only lived thus in the Stone Age and later ages, but there are people living in the same manner in the East Indies and other places at this day), made good use of their stone hatchets, for they not only cut down trees, but killed such animals—and very fierce they were—as the bear, wolf and wild boar. They had learned to fish with nets made of flax, which they floated with buoys of bark, and sank with stone weights.

Besides what we know about the dwellings of men in early times, there have been found on the shores of Denmark, Scotland and elsewhere, enormous heaps of what are called "kitchen-middens." These were really the feeding-places of the people who lived on or about those coasts, and are made up of piles of shells, largely those of the oyster, mussel, periwinkle, &c., on which they fed. With these there have also been found the bones of stags and other animals, and also of birds, as well as flint knives and other things.

I said at starting that the three things which man would first need were food, fire and shelter, and, having told you how these were procured by him, you are perhaps wondering how these people of the Stone Age spoke to each other and what words they used. This we shall never know, but we may be sure that they had some way of making their thoughts known one to another, and that they learned to speak and write and count little by little, just as they learned everything else. They had some idea of drawing, for bones and pieces of slate have been found with rough sketches of the mammoth, bull, and other beasts scratched on them. These old-world pictures witness to the truth, that man is greater than brutes in this as in other things, since no brute has yet been known to draw a picture, write an alphabet, or learn how to make a fire.

But I shall have something to say about speaking and writing by and by.

VII. USE OF METALS.

In course of time, some man, wiser than his fellows, made use of his quicker eye and more active brain to discover the metals which the earth contained; and this marks a great gain, for which we cannot be too thankful. When we think about the thousand different uses to which metals are put—how without them no ship big enough and strong enough to cross the ocean could have been built, or steam-engine to speed us along constructed —we learn how enormous is their value to us. It is certain that if man had never discovered them he would have remained in a savage, or, at least, a barbarous state.

Through all the story of his progress we see that he never went to the storehouse of the earth in vain. Therein were treasured up for him the metals which he needed when stone was found to be too blunt and soft for the work he wished to do; therein the vast coal-beds which were laid open to supply the cosy fires when wood grew scarce.

Gold, which means the *yellow, bright* metal (from *gulr*, yellow), was most likely the first metal used by man. Its glitter would attract his eye, while, unlike some other metals, it is found in rivers, and on various rocks on the surface of the earth. It has to be mixed with another metal to be hard enough for general use; and in its native state would be therefore easily shaped into ornaments. Savage and polished people are alike in this love of ornament. Necklaces of shells and amber made in the Stone Age have been found; and to this day savages think of decoration before dress. One very common way of making themselves smart, as they think, is by marking their face, body, and limbs with curved lines, made with a pointed instrument, filling in the marks with color. This is called tattooing. If this shows that people have in all places and times loved to look fine, although they have gone throng pain and discomfort as the price, it also shows that the love of what is beautiful, or of what is thought to be beautiful, is theirs, and that is another thing which the brute has not. No herds of cows ever leave off feeding to admire a sunset; and you never saw a horse or a monkey with face lit up with delight at the sight of a rainbow.

Copper is a metal which came into early use, as, like gold, it is often found unmixed with anything else, and its softness enables it to be worked into various shapes. Where it was scarce, and tin could be had, fire was made use of to melt and mix the two together, forming the pretty, hard, and useful metal called bronze. By pouring the molten mass into a mould of stone or sand, weapons of the shape wanted would be made.

The age when the metals I have named were used is called the "Age of Bronze." A very long time passed before iron was smelted, that is, melted and got away from the ore (or *vein* running through the rock) with which it is found, because this is very hard work, and needs more skill than men had then; but when they succeeded in smelting and moulding it, it took the place of bronze for making spear-heads, swords, hatchets, &c., bronze being used for the handles and for ornaments, many of which—such as earrings, bracelets, and hair-pins —have been found among the ruins in the Swiss lakes.

Silver and lead were used later still.

You have thus far learnt that by finding river-beds, caverns, and elsewhere, various tools, weapons, ornaments, and other remains, some of them at great depth, and all without doubt made by man, it is known that he must have lived many thousands of years before we have any records of him in histories written on papyrus (which was the reed from which the ancients made their paper— hence the name "paper"), or painted on the walls of tombs.

By the way of marking the steps in man's progress his early history is divided into three periods, named after the things used in them, as thus :—

1. The Age of Stone, which, as stated at page 17, is also divided into the Old Stone Age and the Newer Stone Age.
2. The Age of Bronze.
3. The Age of Iron.

When you can get to the British Museum, go into the room where the "British Antiquities" are kept, and there you will see for yourself the different flint and metal tools and weapons which I have described.

How many years passed between the shaping of the

first flint and the moulding of the first bronze weapon
is not known. We are sure that men used stone before
they used bronze and iron, and that some tribes were in
the Stone Age when other tribes had found out the value
of metals. The three Ages overlap and run into each other
" like the three chief colors of the rainbow."

For example, although some of the lake-dwellings,
about which I have told you, were built by men in the
Stone Age, a very large number belong to the Bronze
Age; and the relics which have been brought to light
show how decided was the progress which man had made
The lake-dwellers had learned to cultivate wheat, to store
up food for winter use, to weave garments of flax, and to
tame the most useful animals, such as the horse, the
sheep and the goat. Man had long before this found out
what a valuable creature the dog is, for the lowest tribes
who lived on the northern sea-coasts have left proof of
this in the bones found among the shell heaps.

In what is known as the Age of Iron very rapid progress was made; and while the variety of pottery, the
casting of bronze coins, the discovery of glass, and
a crowd of other new inventions show what great advance
was made in the *things* man used, they show also how
fast man himself was rising from a low state.

VIII. MAN'S GREAT AGE ON THE EARTH.

At this point of the story you will, perhaps, be asking
a question, to which I will give the best answer that can
at present be found.

You will ask how it is that we know these remains of early man to be so very, very old.

To make my reply as clear as possible, I will describe to you one of the many places in which the old bones and weapons have been found.

There is a large cavern at Brixham, on the south coast of Devonshire, which was discovered fourteen years ago through the falling in of a part of the roof. The floor is of stalagmite, or particles of lime, which have been brought down from the roof by the dropping of water, and become hardened into stone again. *Stalagmite* comes from a Greek word which means a *drop*. In this floor, which is about one foot in thickness, were found bones of the reindeer and cave-bear, while below it was a red loamy mass, fifteen feet thick in some parts, in which were buried flint flakes, or knives, and bones of the mammoth. Beneath this was a bed of gravel, more than twenty feet thick, in which flint flakes and some small bones were found. Altogether, more than thirty flints were found in the same cave with the bones of bears and woolly elephants; and as they are known to have been chipped by the hand of man, it is not hard to prove that he lived in this country when those creatures roamed over it.

But what proof have we, you ask, that the bones of these creatures are so very old? Apart from the fact that for many centuries no living mammoth has been seen, we have the finding of its bones buried at a goodly depth ; and as it is certain that no one would trouble to dig a grave to put them in, there must be some other cause for the mass of loam under which they are found.

There are several ways by which the various bones may have got into the cave. The creatures to which they belonged may have died on the hillside, and their bones have been washed into the cave ; or they may have sought refuge, or, what in the case I am now describing seems most likely, lived therein ; but, be this as it may, we have to account for the thirty-five feet of loam and gravel in which their remains are buried.

The agent that thus covered them from view for long, long years, is that active tool of nature which, before the day when no living thing was upon the earth, and ever since, has been cutting through rocks, opening the deep valleys, shaping the highest mountains, hollowing out the lowest caverns, and which is carrying the soil from one place to another to form new lands where now the deep sea rolls. It is *water* which carried that deposit into Brixham cavern and covered over the bones, and which, since the day that mammoth and bear and reindeer lived in Devonshire, has scooped out the surrounding valleys 100 feet deeper. And although the time which water takes to deepen a channel, or eat out a cavern, depends upon the speed with which it flows, you may judge that the quickest stream works slowly to those who watch it, when I tell you that the river Thames, flowing at its present rate, takes eleven thousand seven hundred and forty years to scoop out *its* valley *one foot* lower! Men of science have therefore some reason for believing that the flint weapons were made by men who lived many thousands of years ago.

" A thousand years in Thy sight are but as yesterday when it is past, and as a watch in the night."

Science, in thus teaching us the great age of the earth, also teaches us the Eternity of the Ageless God; and likewise those vast distances about which astronomers tell us make the universe seem a fitter temple for Him to dwell in than did the old, cramped notions of a flat earth, for whose benefit alone the sun shed his light by day, and the moon and stars their light by night. Science illumines with new beauty the grand thoughts of the starwatching poet of old, who sang, " If I ascend up into heaven, Thou art there; if I make my bed in the unseen world, behold, Thou art there."

IX. MANKIND AS SHEPHERDS, FARMERS, TRADERS.

From being a roving, wild, long-haired savage, gnawing roots, or crouching behind rock or tree to pounce upon his prey, uncertain each morning whether night would not set in before he could get enough to eat, man had become a shepherd or tiller of the soil, not only learning the greatness of the earth in which he had been placed, but also beginning dimly to feel his own greatness above the beast of the field and the fowl of the air.

Some part of mankind, finding how useful certain animals were for the milk and flesh which they gave as food, and for the skins, especially of their young ones, which could be made into soft clothing, had learned to tame and gather them into flocks and herds, moving with them from place to place wherever the most grass could be had. These men were the first shepherds or herdsmen, living a nomad (which means *wandering*) life, dwelling in tents because they could be easily removed.

This was the kind of life that Abraham lived thousands of years ago, and that the Arabs and other wandering tribes still live at this day.

While some loved the shepherd's or herdsman's life, others chose a more settled state, becoming farmers or tillers of the earth. The word earth means the *plowed*.

To do this work well, the rude stone implements of their forefathers were useless, and implements made of the best and hardest metals were needed. Then, as they remained in one place, they would not be content with log huts as men were in the Stone Age, or with tents as the nomads were, but would have their houses well built, with places like stables and barns in which to lodge their cattle and store up their corn.

All the sunny days would be wanted for their field-work, and they would therefore be glad to employ others who could build their houses and make their tools. Thus one after another different trades would arise and be carried on, which would bring people together for mutual help and gain ; thus houses would multiply into villages, villages would become towns, and towns would grow into cities.

The different classes of people would unite together for protection against their enemies, and either all would learn the art of war, or would select some of the bravest and strongest among them to become the army to defend the land. Some one man, the best and ablest they could find, would be chosen to carry out the laws which the people agreed to make for the well-being of all.

For in early as well as in later times, the bad passions and jealousies of men broke out and caused those desolating wars which have darkened so many bright spots in this world. It is certain that the tillers of the soil and the dwellers in towns would be more inclined to a peaceful and quiet life than the roving tribes or their chieftain with his followers and herds and flocks, who would often seek to gain by force what they coveted.

Not that these were always to blame, but they would be the more likely of the two to " pick a quarrel." Disputes arose between them about the ownership of the land ; the nomads, who loved the lazy ease of a pastoral life more than the hard work of tool-making or house-building, would want to share some of the good fruits which the farmers were making the earth to yield, or some of the bright, sharp edged weapons which the metal-workers were moulding, and in various ways "bad blood," as people call it, would be stirred, which would end in fighting. The stronger would conquer the weaker, seize upon or lay waste their land, and make slaves of such of the prisoners as they thought it worth while to spare. It was an age, like many ages since, when no tender feelings ruled in the heart of man, but when the "golden rule" was not, and the harsh, stern law was this:

> "That they shall take who have the power,
> And they shall keep who can."

But wars do not last for ever, and men would find that it was, after all, better to live in friendship and peace. So they would trade together; the earth would yield the farmer more food than he needed, and he would be glad to barter with it, giving some of it to the herdsman in exchange for cattle, and to the toolmaker in exchange for tools, each of whom would be very glad to trade with him.

Then as bartering grew, it was found very awkward and cumbersome to carry things from place to place, especially if they were now and then not very much wanted, and people would agree to make use of something which was handy to carry, steady in value, and that did not spoil by keeping. So, whenever they could, men fixed upon pieces of metal, first casting bronze into coins, and then using gold and silver, which being scarcer than other metals are worth more. We learn from the paintings at Thebes, and from ancient history, that gold and silver were counted as wealth in early times. Abraham is said in the Book of Genesis (which you will read when you are older) to have been "very rich in cattle, in silver, and in gold." The word "pecuniary," which is used in speaking of a man's riches, comes from the Latin word *pecus*, which means *cattle*, and shows that formerly a man's wealth was sometimes reckoned by the cattle he had. Another proof of the meaning that a word will hold.

And this reminds me that I have to tell you a little about speaking, writing, and counting.

X. LANGUAGE.

In what way the wonderful gift of language came to man we do not know, and the wise of many ages have tried in vain to find out.

The same God who made the beautiful organs in man by which he can utter so many different sounds, gave him the power of creating names for the things which he saw, and words for the thought which dwelt in his mind.

There are some words which we can account for, such as those which imitate sounds, as when we say the clock "ticks," or call the "cuckoo" and the "peewit" after the sound they make. But this explains only a portion of the vast number of words which make up a language, and which spring from roots deep down, too deep for us to track.

Man at first had very few words, and those were short

ones, and in making known his thoughts to others, he used signs very much; "gesture language," as it has been called. We do the same now; for in shaking the head to mean "no," in nodding it to mean "yes," and in shaking hands in proof that we are joined in friendship, we speak in gesture-language, and would have to do it a great deal if we were traveling in some country of which we did not know the language.

There are very few things that cannot be expressed by signs or gestures, and among the ancients entire plays were performed by persons called pantomimes (which word means *imitators of all things*), who acted not by speaking, but wholly by mimicry.

A story is told of a king who was in Rome when Nero was emperor, and who, having seen the wonderful mimicry of a pantomime begged him as a present, so that he might make use of him to have dealings with the nations whose languages he did not know. We have now so many words that we need use signs but very little, if at all.

Just as all the races of mankind are thought to have come from one family, so the different languages which they speak are thought to have flowed from one source.

There are *three* leading streams of language, and I shall have to quote a few hard names in telling you about them.

It was thought some years ago that Hebrew, which is the language in which the sacred books of the Jews (known to us as the Old Testament) are written, was the parent, so to speak, of all other languages, but it has since been found through tracing words to their early forms that

1. Sanskrit, in which the sacred books of the Brahmans are written, and which was a spoken tongue in the time of Solomon and Alexander the Great, but which has been a "dead" or unspoken language for more than two thousand years;

    Zend, in which the sacred books of the Parsees (or so-called fire-worshipers) are written;

    Greek, the language of Greece;

    Latin, the language of the ancient Romans;

and nearly all the other dialects and languages of India and Europe, are children of the Indo-European, or Aryan family.

I told you something about these Aryans at page 13, and will add that through their language we know that they had learned "the arts of plowing and making roads, of sewing and weaving, of building houses, and of counting as far as one hundred." The ties of father, mother, brother, and sister, were hallowed among them, and they called upon God, who "is Light," by the name still heard in Christian churches and Indian temples. That name is *Deity*. It comes from a very ancient word by which these people spoke of the *sky*, and which was afterwards applied to Him who dwells in the sky. For "beyond sun, and moon, and stars, and all which changes, and will change, was the clear blue sky, the boundless firmament of heaven." There man in every age has fixed the dwelling-place of God who is Light, and in whom is no darkness at all.

2. The second division of languages includes the Hebrew; the Arabic, in which the Koran, the sacred book of the Mohammedans, is written; and the languages on the very old monuments of Phœnicia, Babylon, Assyria, and Carthage.

3. The third division includes the remaining languages of Asia, with the exception of the Chinese, which stands by itself as the only relic of the first forms of human speech, being made up of words of one syllable.

The ancient language of Britain is now found only in some parts of Wales, Ireland, and Scotland, and the foundation of our present language, which now contains above one hundred thousand words, is the same as that spoken on the coast of Germany. It was brought over by Angles, Saxons (hence Anglo-Saxons), Jutes and other tribes from the Continent. Anglo-Saxon is the mother-tongue of our present English, to which in various forms Latin words have been added, together with a few words from the languages of other nations.

For teaching you the different changes in the English language, as well as for an interesting list of words borrowed from the Arabic, Turkish, Chinese, &c., the best books to help you are Dr. Morris's "Historical Outlines of English Accidence," and Archbishop Trench's " English Past and Present."

I am afraid I have confused you a little in this talk about language, but you can hear it another time over again when you are older and better able to learn the importance belonging to the study of the wonderful gift by which we are able to talk to people in various languages, and read in ancient books the history of man's gropings after God. I want to lead you on to feel and know that the study of words is a delightful way of spending time, and that the dictionary, which is thought by most people to be a dry book, is full of poetry and history locked up in its words, which the key of the wise will open.

XI. WRITING.

It is much easier to tell you how men learned to write.

The use of writing is to put something before the eye in such a way that its meaning may be known at a glance, and the earliest way of doing this was by a picture. Picture-writing was thus used for many ages, and is still found among savage races in all quarters of the globe. On rocks, stone slabs, trees, and tombs, this way was employed to record an event, or tell some message.

In the course of time, instead of this tedious mode,

men learned to write signs for certain words or sounds. Then the next step was to separate the word into letters, and to agree upon certain signs to always represent certain letters, and hence arose alphabets. The shape of the letters of the alphabet is thought by some to bear traces of the early picture-writing. To show you what is meant, Aleph, the first letter of the Hebrew alphabet, means an *ox*, and the sign for that letter was an outline of an *ox's head*.

The signs used by astronomers for the sun, moon and planets; the signs I, II, III, for one, two, and three, are proofs that if picture-writing is of value to man in a civilized state, it must have been of greater value to him, and much more used by him the farther we search back. We still speak of *signing* our name, although we have ceased to use a sign or mark, as was done when few could write.

XII. COUNTING.

The art of Counting is slowly learned by savage tribes, and at this day some are found that cannot reckon beyond four, or that, if they can, have no words for higher figures.

All over the world the fingers have been and are used as counters, and among many tribes the word for "hand" and "five" is the same.

This may be taken as a common mode by which the savage reckons:

One hand 5
Two hands or half a man . . . 10
Two hands, and one foot . . 15
Hands and feet, or one man - . . 20

We do the same, as shown in the word *digit*, which is the name for any of the figures from one to nine, and comes from the Latin *digitus*, which means a *finger;* while counting by fives and tens enters into all our dealings. One early way of counting was by pebbles, the Latin for which is *calculi*, and we preserve this fact in our use of the word *calculate*; just as, when we tie a knot in our handkerchief to remind us of something we fear to forget, we are copying the ancient plan of counting with knotted cords.

This story of the World's Childhood has been chiefly learned by studying the lessons taught by those traces of man which are found in the north-western part of Europe, but it is believed that he first lived elsewhere, and afterwards traveled here. For in the days known as the Ancient Stone Age, when Britain and Ireland were joined to the main land, and great rivers flowed through the valleys which are now covered by the German Ocean and English Channel, and when woolly-haired elephants and rhinoceroses roamed about in the pine forests of what is now England and France, Europe was very much colder than it is now, and it is thought that man did not live there before these huge creatures.

You will one day learn from the beautiful story which

rocks and rivers are ever telling, what vast changes have
happened over all the earth, in proof of which you may
think about what I have already said, to which may be
added, that the sea once swept over the place where you
live, and ages hence may flow over it again.

XIII. MAN'S WANDERINGS FROM HIS FIRST HOME.

It is believed that man lived at first somewhere near
the middle of Asia, and from thence those who came after
him spread on all sides, some settling in the rich plains
watered by the river Nile, to become the forefathers of
Egyptian kings, others wandering to the bleak shores of
Northern Europe to become the forefathers of the Sea-
kings.

As the climate in which people live affects the color of
their skins, so the progress of any race, as well as the
kind of life which they live, depend very much on the
land they dwell in, and this will explain why some races
have progressed so much more than others, and even become their rulers. Where there were rich, grassy plains,
the people gathered flocks and herds, wandered from
place to place in search of good pasture, and made scarcely any advance. Where a fruitful soil and balmy air
were to be had, there people would settle as farmers and
workers in wood and metals, gathering both knowledge
and wealth, while those who lived on islands and by the
sea-coasts became adventurous and bold.

It is not the object of this narrative to take you beyond the time when histories usually begin, and what you
have learned does not therefore relate to any single tribe
or nation, but to the growth of mankind as a whole. I
will, however, sketch in a few lines the course which the
leading races of mankind took after they left their supposed common home.

The tribes who wandered into the northern parts of
Europe lived for ages a wild roving life; and when they
had so far advanced as to find out, or, what is more likely, learn from other races, the use of metals, and then to
apply their powers in building ships stout and strong
enough to brave the open sea, they became the terror of
quiet people, and you will learn from old English history
how they pounced one after another upon this island,
plundering wherever and whatever they could.

Other tribes settled down in Persia; on the sea-board
of Palestine; in Egypt; and were the roots from which
grew those mighty nations whose kings had reigned for
many years before the birth of Abraham. Other tribes
leapt across the narrow straits between Asia and America,
and wandered over that vast New World, those who
traveled southwards becoming builders of cities whose
ruins tell of their past importance.

Long before the great empires of Greece and Rome,
there arose a people known to us as the Jews, whose history fills so many books of the Bible, and who were de-
scended from a chieftain named Abraham. I shall have

some interesting stories to tell you further on concerning this good and noble man.

Abraham left his native land and moved with his slaves and cattle to Palestine. His descendants afterwards settled in Egypt, which was then a great corn-yielding country, where they grew to large numbers, and were treated kindly during the lifetime of Joseph, whose touching story is told in the Book of Genesis. After his death they were, however, made slaves and used very harshly. A good, learned, and heroic man named Moses, who, although he had been brought up by the king's daughter as her son, burned with righteous anger for the wrongs of his oppressed countrymen, rose at the head of them and delivered them. How they journeyed to Palestine, living under chiefs or judges; killing, in the cruel manner of that age, men, women, and children; how they grew and prospered, but, falling into vice, became weak and enslaved: then rose again for a time, until when Jesus Christ lived they were subject to the Roman Empire, you will learn by and by from Scripture histories.

XIV. MAN'S PROGRESS IN ALL THINGS.

The early history of man shows us how wonderful his progress has been when we compare the Age of Stone with our present happy lot. Not only in house-building, cooking, pottery, clothing, various uses of metals, have rude ways been improved upon, but also in his knowledge of the earth beneath and the stars around has the progress of man been vast. The lightning and the wind, the rushing stream, daily work for him, and their force is chained to do his bidding. He has already seen a good depth, and may see further yet, into the mystery of the stars, and every day he is spelling out some sentence here and there in the great book of Nature.

One would like to know and thank those men of the past who laid the foundation of all that has since been done. For he who first chipped a flint was the father of all sculptors ; he who first scratched a picture of man or mammoth was the father of all painters ; he who first piled stones together was the father of all builders of abbeys and cathedrals ; he who first bored a hole in a reindeer's bone to make a whistle, or twanged a stretched sinew, was the father of all musicians ; he who first rhymed his simple thoughts was the father of all poets ; he who first strove to learn the secret of sun and star was the father of all astronomers.

XV.   DECAY OF PEOPLES.

I have called this "simple account of man in early times" by the title of the " Childhood of the World," because the progress of the world from its past to its present state is like the growth of each of us from childhood to manhood or womanhood.

Although the story has, on the whole, flowed smoothly along, we must not leave out of sight the terrible facts which have sometimes checked the current. History, in

books and in ruins, teaches that there have been tribes
and nations (some of the nations so great and splendid
that it seemed impossible for them ever to fall) which
have reached a certain point, they decayed and died.
And since man has lived so many thousands of years on
the earth, there must have risen and fallen races and
tribes of which no trace will ever be found.

The cause of the shameful sin and crime of which
every place in this world has been more or less the scene,
has sometimes been man's ignorance of what is due to
his God and his fellow-man, but more often his willful
use of power to do evil, forgetting, in his folly and
wrong-doing, that the laws of God change not, that Sin
is a fair-dealing master and pays his servants the wages
of death. They have disobeyed the law of love, and
hence have arisen cruel wars and shocking butcheries;
captures of free people and the crushing of their brave
spirits in slavery. They have disobeyed the laws of
health, and the plague or "black death" has killed tens
of thousands, or gluttony and drunkenness have destroyed them. They have loved money and selfish ease (forgetting the eternal fact that not one of us can live by
bread alone, but that we live our lowest if that be the
end and aim of our life), and their souls, lean and
hungry, have perished.

But although the hand on the clock-face of progress
has seemed now and then to stand still, or even to go
back, it is a great truth for our comfort and trust that

the world gets better and not worse. There are some people who are always sighing for what is not or cannot be; who look back to the days of their childhood and wish them here again; who are ever talking of the "good old days" when laughter rang with richest mirth, when work was plentiful and beggars scarce, and life so free from care that wrinkles never marked the happy face. Do not listen to these people; they have either misread the past or not read it at all. Like some other things, it is well-looking at a distance, but ill-looking near. We have not to go far back to the "good old times," to learn that kings and queens were worse lodged and fed and taught than a servant is nowadays.

It is very foolish and wrong to either wish the past back again, or to speak slightingly of it. It filled its place; it did its appointed work. Even out of terrible wars blessings have sometimes come, and that which men have looked upon as evil has been fruitful in good. We cannot see the end as well as the beginning : God alone can do that. The true wisdom is to see in all the steps of this earth's progress the guiding hand of God, and to believe that He will not leave to itself the world which for His own pleasure he has created. For

"nothing walks with aimless feet."

To you and to every one of us, God gives work to do; and if He takes it away, it is that others may do it better, and so the well-being of all be secured.

Let us strive to do thoroughly the work which we find

nearest to our hand ; though we may think it small and trifling, it is not so in the sight of Him who made the dew-drop as well as the sun, and who looks not so much upon the thing we have to do, as upon the way and the spirit in which we do it.

———

PART II.

XVI. INTRODUCTORY.

In seeking to show you by what slow steps man came to believe in one all-wise and all-good God, I wish to fix one great truth upon your young heart about Him ; for the nobler your view of Him is, the nobler is your life likely to be.

Now you would think your father very hard and cruel if he loaded you with all the good things he had, and sent your brothers and sisters, each of them yearning for his love and kisses, to some homeless spot to live uncared for and unloved, and to die unwept.

And yet this is exactly what some people have said that God does. They have spoken of Him, who has given life to every man, woman, and child, without power on their part to take or refuse what is thus given, as being near only a few of His creatures, and leaving the rest, feeling a soul-hunger after Him, to care for themselves and to never find Him.

Believe that He who is called our Father is better, more just, more loving, than the best fathers can be, and that He " is not far from any one of us."

In those dim ages through which I have led you, God, whose breath made and ever makes each of us " a living soul," was as near the people who lived then as He is near us, leading them, although they, like ourselves, often knew it not. The rudest, and to us in some things most shocking, forms of religion, were not invented by any devil, permitted by God to delude men to destruction, but were, as we learn from savage races now, the early struggles of man from darkness to twilight—for no man really loves the darkness—and from twilight to full day.

Around him was the beauty and motion of life ; before him very often the mystery of death, for there were weeping fathers and mothers in those old times over dead little children, and friends stood silent and tearful beside their dead friends in those days as they do in these ; and do you think that man would sit himself down to frame a willful, cunning lie about the things which awed him ?

Although the ideas which these early men had about what they saw and felt were wrong, *they were right to them*, and it was only after a long time when some shrewd man, making bad use of his shrewdness, pretended to know more than God will ever permit man to know here, that lies and juggling with the truth of things began.

I tell you this because I want you to feel a trust in God
that nothing can take away; and how much you will
need this trust, when your heart comes to feel the sin and
sorrow of this world, the years that are before you will
reveal.

XVII. MAN'S FIRST QUESTIONS.

It was not long after man had risen from his first low
state, and the chief wants of his body were supplied, that
he would begin to act the *man* still more by *thinking*
(see page 12), and then would hear some voice within,
telling him that eating and drinking were not the chief
ends for which life had been given him.

He saw around him the world with its great silent hills
and green valleys; its rugged ridges of purple-tinted
mountains, and miles of barren flat; its trees and fra-
grant flowers; the graceful forms of man, the soaring
bird, the swift deer and kingly lion; the big, ungainly-
shaped mammoth, long since died out; the wide scene,
beaming with the colors which came forth at the bidding touch of the sunlight, or bathed in the shadows
cast by passing clouds; he saw the sun rise and travel to
the west, carrying the light away; the moon at regular
times growing from sickle-shape to full round orb; *
then each night the stars, few or many, bursting out like
sparks struck off the wheels of the Sun-God's chariot, or

* Moon means the *measurer*, hence our word *month*, "for time was measured by nights and moons long before it was reckoned by days and suns
and years."

like the glittering sprays of water cast by a ship as she plows the sea.

His ears listened to the different sounds of Nature; the music of the flowing river; the roar of the never-silent sea; the rustle of the leaves as they were swept by the unseen fingers of the breeze; the patter of the rain as it dropped from the great black clouds; the rumble of the thunder as it followed the spear-like flashes of light sent from the rolling clouds: these and a hundred other sounds, now harsh, now sweet, made him ask— What does it all mean? Where and what am I? Whence came I; whence came all that I see and hear and touch?

Man's first feeling was one of simple wonder; his second feeling the wish to find out the *cause* of things, what it was that made them as they were.

All around him was Nature (by which is meant *that which brings forth*), great, mighty, beautiful; was it not all alive, for did it not all move?

In thinking how man would seek to get at the cause of what he saw, we must not suppose that he could reason as we do. But although he could not shape his thoughts into polished speech, common sense stood by to help him.

He knew that he himself moved or stood still as he chose, that his choice was ruled by certain reasons, and that only when he willed to do anything was it done. Something within governed all that he did. Nature was not still ; the river flowed, the clouds drifted, the leaves trembled, the earth shook; sun, moon, and stars stayed not : these then must be moved by something within them.

Thus began a belief in spirits dwelling in everything —in sun, tree, waterfall, flame, beast, bird, and serpent.

XVIII. MYTHS.

In seeking to account for the kind of life which seemed to be (and really was, although not as he thought of it) in all things around, man shaped the most curious notions into the form of *myths*, by which is meant a fanciful story founded on something real. If to us a boat or a ship becomes a sort of personal thing, especially when named after anyone ; if " Jack Frost," and " Old Father Christmas," which are but names, seem also persons to the mind of a little child, we may readily see how natural it is for savages to think that the flame licking up the wood is a living thing whose head could be cut off; to believe that the gnawing feeling of hunger is caused by a lizard or a bird in the stomach ; to imagine that the echoes which the hills threw back came from the dwarfs who dwelt among them, and that the thunder was the rumbling of the Heaven-God's chariot wheels.

Myths have changed their form in different ages, but they remain among us even now, and live in many a word still used, the first meaning of which has died out. To show you what is meant : we often speak of a cross

or sullèn person being in a bad *humor*, which word rests
on a very old and false notion that there were four moist-
ures or *humors* in the body, on the proper mixing of
which the good or bad temper of a person depended.

In telling you a little about myths I cannot attempt
to show you where the simple early myths become later
on stiffened into the legends of heroes, with loves and
fears and hates and mighty deeds, such as make up so
much of the early history of Greece and Rome, for that
you will learn from other and larger books than this.

XIX. MYTHS ABOUT SUN AND MOON.

Among many savage tribes, the sun and moon are
thought to be man and wife, or brother and sister. One
of the most curious myths of this kind comes from the
Esquimaux, the dwellers in the far North. It relates that
when a girl was at a party, some one told his love for
her by shaking her shoulders after the manner of the
country. She could not see who it was in the dark hut,
so she smeared her hands with soot, and when he came
back she blackened his cheek with her hand. When a
light was brought she saw that it was her brother, and
fled. He ran after her and followed her as she came to
the end of the earth and sprang out into the sky. There
she became the sun and he the moon, and this is why the
moon is always chasing the sun through the heavens, and
why the moon is sometimes dark as he turns his blackened cheek towards the earth.

In all the languages known as Teutonic the moon was of the male gender and the sun of the female gender.

Among other people, and in later times, the sun is spoken of as the lover of the dawn, who went before him, killing her with his bright spear-like rays, while night was a living thing which swallowed up the day. If the sun is a face streaming with locks of light, the moon is a silver boat, or a mermaid living half her time under the water. When the sun shone with a pleasant warmth he was called the friend of man ; when his heat scorched the earth he was said to be slaying his children. You have perhaps heard that the dark patches on the moon's face, which look so very much like a nose and two eyes, gave rise to the notion of a " man in the moon," who was said to be set up there for picking sticks on a Sunday.

XX. MYTHS ABOUT ECLIPSES.

There is something so weird and gloomy in eclipses of the sun and moon, that we can readily understand how through all the world they have been looked upon as the direct work of some dreadful power.

The Chinese imagine them to be caused by great dragons trying to devour the sun and moon, and beat drums and brass kettles to make the monsters give up their prey. Some of the tribes of American Indians speak of the moon as hunted by huge dogs, catching and tearing her till her soft light is reddened and put out by the blood flowing from her wounds. To this day in India the native beats his going as the moon passes across the sun's face, and it is not so very long ago that in Europe both eclipses and rushing comets were thought to show that troubles were near.

Fear is the daughter of Ignorance, and departs when knowledge enlightens us as to the cause of things.

We know that an eclipse (which comes from Greek words meaning *to leave out* or *forsake*) is caused either by the moon passing in such a line between the earth and the sun as to cause his light to be in part or altogether hidden, *left out* for a short time, or by the earth so passing between the sun and moon as to throw its shadow upon the moon and partly or wholly hide her light. *Our* fear would arise if eclipses did not happen at the very moment when astronomers have calculated them to occur.

XXI. MYTHS ABOUT STARS.

There is a curious Asian myth about the stars which tells that the sun and moon are both women. The stars are the moon's children, and the sun once had as many. Fearing that mankind could not bear so much light, each agreed to eat up her children. The moon hid hers away, but the sun kept her word, which no sooner had she done than the moon brought her children from their hiding-place. When the sun saw them she was filled with rage, and chased the moon to kill her, and the chase has lasted ever since. Sometimes the sun comes

near enough to bite the moon, and that is an eclipse.
The sun, as men may still see, devours her stars at dawn,
but the moon hides hers all day while the sun is near,
and brings them out at night only, when the sun is far
away.

The names still in use for certain clusters of stars and
single stars, were given long ago when the stars were
thought to be living creatures. They were said to be
men who had once lived here, or to be mighty hunters
or groups of young men and maidens dancing. Many of
the names given show that the stars were watched with
anxiety by the farmer and sailor, who thought they ruled
the weather. The group of stars known to us as the Plei-
ades were so called from the word *plain*, which means to
sail, because the old Greek sailors watched for their rising
before they ventured on the ocean. The same stars are
called the *digging* stars by the Zulus, who live in South
Africa, because when they appear the people begin to
dig. A very good illustration of the change which a
myth takes is afforded by these same stars, which are
spoken of in Greek mythology as the seven daughters of
Atlas (who was said to bear the world on his shoulders),
six of whom were wedded to the Gods, but the seventh
to a king, for which reason Merope, as she is named,
shines the faintest of them all.

The stars were formerly believed to govern the fate of
a person in life. The temper was said to be good or bad,
the nature grave or gay, according to the planet which

was in the ascendant, as it was called, at birth. Several words in our language witness to this old belief. We speak of a " disaster," which means the stroke or blast of an unlucky star ; *aster* being a Greek word for *star*. We call a person " ill-starred " or " born under a lucky star." Grave and gloomy people are called "saturnine," because those born under the planet Saturn are said to be so disposed. Merry and happy-natured people are called " jovial," as born under the planet Jupiter, or Jove. Active and sprightly people are called "mercurial," as born under the planet Mercury. Mad people are called " lunatics." *Luna* is the Latin word for moon, and the more sane movements of the insane were believed to depend upon her phases or appearances of change in form.

Sun, moon, and stars were all thought to be fixed to the great heavens (which means *heaved* or lifted up, and comes from an Anglo-Saxon word, *hefan*, to lift), because it seemed like a solid arch over the flat earth. To many a mind it was the place of bliss, where care and want and age could never enter. The path to it was said to be along that bright-looking band across the sky known to us as the " Milky Way," the sight of which has given birth to several beautiful myths. I should like to stay and tell you some of them, but we must not let the myths keep us too long from the realities.

XXII. MYTHS ABOUT THE EARTH AND MAN.

The waterspout was thought to be a giant or sea-serpent reaching from sea to sky; the rainbow (which books about light will tell you is a circle, half only of which we can see) was said to be a living demon coming down to drink when the rain fell, or, prettier myth, the heaven-ladder or bridge along which the souls of the blest are led by angels to Paradise, or the bow of God set in the clouds, as Indian, Jew, and Fin have called it; the clouds were cows driven by the children of the morning to their pasture in the blue fields of heaven; the tides were the beating of the ocean's heart; the earthquake was caused by the Earth-Tortoise moving underneath; the lightning was the forked tongue of the storm-demon, the thunder was his roar; volcanoes were the dwelling-places of angry demons who threw up red-hot stones from them.

Man's sense of the wonderful is so strong that a belief in giants and pigmies and fairies was as easy to him as it has been hard to remove. The bones of huge beasts now extinct were said to have belonged to giants, whose footprints were left in those hollows in stones which we know to be water-worn. The big loose stones were said to have been torn from the rocks by the giants and hurled at their foes in battle. The stories of the very small people who once lived in this part of Europe, and whose descendants now live in Lapland, gave rise

a belief in dwarfs. The flint arrow-heads of the Stone
Age were said to be elf-darts used by the little spirits
dwelling in woods and wild places, while the polished
stone axes were thunderbolts.

How all kinds of other myths, such as those accounting
for the bear's stumpy tail, the robin's red breast, the
crossbill's twisted bill, the aspen's quivering leaf, arose,
I cannot now stay to tell you, nor how out of myths
there grew the nursery stories and fairy tales which children never tire of hearing; for we must now be starting on
our voyage from the wonderful realm of fancy to the not
less wonderful land of fact, whither science is ever bearing us. Nay, not less wonderful but more wonderful,
since the fancies come from the facts, not the facts from
the fancies.

XXIII. MAN'S IDEAS ABOUT THE SOUL.

We have learnt that because man saw all nature to be
in motion, he believed that life dwelt in all, that a spirit
moved leaf, and cloud, and beast. *Words* now come in to
tell us what in the course of time was man's notion about
a spirit. The difference between a living and a dead
man is this: the living man breathes and moves; the
dead man has ceased to breathe and is still. Now the
word *spirit* means *breath*, and in the leading languages
of the world the word used for *soul* or *spirit* is that
which signifies *breath* or *wind*. Frequently the soul of
man is thought to be a sort of steam or vapor, or a

man's shadow, which becoming unsettled causes him to
be ill. The savage thinks that the spirit can leave the
body during sleep, and so whatever happens to him in
his dreams seems as real and true as if it had taken
place while he was awake. If he sees some dead friend
in his sleep, he believes either that the dead have come
to him or that his spirit has been on a visit to his friend,
and he is very careful not to wake anyone sleeping lest
the soul should happen to be away from the body. Believing that a man's soul could thus go in and out of his
body, it was also thought that demons could be drawn
in with the breath, and that yawning and sneezing were
proofs of their nearness. So what is called an invocation
was spoken to ward them off, of which we have a trace
in the custom of saying " God bless you " when anyone
sneezes.   .

According to an old Jewish legend, " The custom of
saying ' God bless you ' when a person sneezes dates
from Jacob. The Rabbis say that before the time that
Jacob lived, men sneezed once and that was the end of
them—the shock slew them. This law was set aside at
the prayer of Jacob on condition that in all nations a
sneeze should be hallowed by the words ' God bless
you.' "

Diseases were said to be caused, among other things,
by the soul staying away too long from the body, and
the bringing of it back is a part of the priest's or wizard's
work.

All these ideas, crude as they are, have lived on among people long after they have risen from savagery, and in fact remain among us, although their first meaning is hidden, in such sayings as a man being "out of his mind," or "beside himself," or "come to himself." If the body has suffered any loss in limb or otherwise, the soul is thought to be maimed too. And the belief that it will need, after it leaves the body, all the things which it has had here will explain the custom of killing wives and slaves to follow the deceased, and as among very low races lifeless things are said to have souls, of placing clothes, weapons, and ornaments in the grave for the dead person's use in another world. It is within a very few years that in Europe the soldier's horse that follows his dead master in the funeral procession was shot and buried with him.

Man regarding himself as surrounded by spirits, dwelling in everything and all-powerful to do him good or harm, shaped his notions about them as they seemed to smile or frown upon him.

Not only did he look upon sickness as often the work of demon-spirits, but in his fear he filled the darkness with ghosts of the dead rising from their graves, shrieking at his door, sitting in his house, tapping him on the shoulder, and breaking the silence with their whistling tones.

XXIV. BELIEF IN MAGIC AND WITCHCRAFT.

In the desire to ward off these unwelcome guests, man has made use of charms and magic arts and tricks of different sorts. And there have always been those who, shrewder than the rest, have traded on the fears of the weak and timid, and professed to have power over the spirits or such influence with them as to drive them away by certain words or things. Medicine-men, rain-makers, wizards, conjurers, and sorcerers, these have abounded everywhere; and even among us now there are found, under other names, people who think they have power with the unseen and know more about the unknown than has ever been or will be given to man to find out in this life.

This belief in magical arts, which is so firmly rooted among the lowest tribes of mankind, has only within the last two hundred years died out among civilized people, and even lingers still in out-of-the-way places among the foolish and ignorant, who are always ready to see a miracle in everything that they cannot understand. Out of it grew the horrid belief in witchcraft, through which it is reckoned *nine millions* of people have been burned? Witchcraft spread with a belief in the devil, who, being looked upon as the enemy of God and man, was regarded as the cause of all the evil in the world, which he worked either by himself or by the aid of agents. It was held that persons had sold themselves to him, he in return

promising that they should lack nothing and should
have power to torment man and woman and child and
beast. If anyone, therefore, felt strange pains—if any
sad loss came—it was the unholy work of witches. It was
they who caused the withering storm ; the ruin to the
crops ; the sudden death of the cattle; and when anyone pined away in sickness, it was because some old
witch had cast her evil eye upon him, or made a waxen
image of him and set it before the fire, that the sick man
may waste away as it melted. The poor creatures who
were charged with thus being in league with the devil
were sought for among helpless old women. To have a
wrinkled face, a hairy lip, a squint eye, a hobbling gait,
a squeaking voice, a scolding tongue ; to live alone :
these were thought proofs enough, and to such miserable
victims torture was applied so cruelly that death was a
welcome release.

XXV. MAN'S AWE OF THE UNKNOWN.

Since all that puzzles the savage puzzles us, we can
feel with him, when he speaks of the soul as breath, of
dreams as real, and, in hushed voice, of good and bad
spirits around.

To this day we have not, nor does it seem likely we
ever can have, any clear idea about the soul. We have
a vague notion that at death it leaves the body as a sort
of filmy thing or shadow or vapor. English, Chinese,
and Indians alike will keep some door or window open

through which the departing soul may leave, and it is a German saying that a door should not be slammed lest a soul be pinched in it!

And our dreams, which so many believe in as bringing faithful messages of joy and sorrow, seem to us so real and "true while they last." Even in the most foolish and baseless stories which are told about bells rung in haunted houses, and ghosts with sheeted arms in church-yards, there is, remember, a witness to the awe in which man, both civilized and savage, in every age and place, holds the unseen.

For all that science tells us about the creatures that teem in a drop of water and in the little bodies that course with our blood, brings us no nearer the great mystery of life. The more powerful the microscopes we use, the more wonders—as we might rightly expect—do we see: but *life itself* no glass will ever show us, and the soul of man no finger will ever touch.

God has given to man a mind, that is, power to think and reason and remember, and with it time, place, and wish to use the gift. He, in the words of a great poet, " wraps man in darkness and makes him ever long for light." As that which costs little is valued little, man would not have cared, had much knowledge been granted him at first, to strive after more; but because he knows little, yet feels that he has the power to learn much, he uses the power in gaining increase of wisdom and knowledge, till he feels the truth of those very old words which say of wisdom, "She is more precious than rubies, and all the things thou canst desire are not to be compared unto her."

XXVI. FETISH-WORSHIP.

So far then we have seen how man seeks to explain what he sees around him, and the next thing we have to find out is, what is his first feeling towards it all? It is to bow before it and worship the powers which seem stronger than himself.

The very lowest form of worship is that paid to life-less things in which some virtue or charm is thought to dwell, and is called " fetish" worship, from a word mean-ing a *charm*. It does not matter what the object is ; it may be a stone of curious shape, the stump of a tree with the roots turned up, even an old hat or a red rag, so long as some good is supposed to be had, or some evil to be thwarted, through it. The worship of stones, about which we may read in the Bible, prevails to this day among rude tribes, who have the strangest notions about them as being sometimes husbands and wives, sometimes the dwelling-place of spirits. The confused ideas which cause the savage to look upon dreams as real cause him to confound the lifeless with the living, and to carefully destroy the parings off his nails and cuttings of his hair, lest evil should be worked through them. The New Zealander would thrust pebbles down the throat of a male child to make its heart hard. The Zulu chews wood

that the heart of his foe or of the woman whom he loves
may soften towards him even as the wood is being bruised.
The dreadful practice of men eating human flesh is supposed to have arisen from the idea that if the flesh of
some strong, brave man be eaten, it makes the eater
strong and brave also. The natives of Borneo will not
eat deer lest they should thereby become faint-hearted,
and the Malays will give much for the flesh of the tiger
to make them brave. If a Tartar doctor has not the
medicine which he wants he will write its name on a
scrap of paper and make a pill of it for the patient to
take. A story is told of a man in Africa who was
thought very holy, and who earned his living by writing
prayers on a board, washing them off and selling the
water.

We may laugh at this, but whenever we say a verse
out of the Bible, or gabble over the beautiful Lord's
Prayer, because we think that in some mysterious way
we get good by so doing, we are fetish-worshipers, and
far below the poor savages I am telling you about, for we
know that unless our hearts speak, no muttering of words
can help us.

XXVII. IDOLATRY.

The customs of worshiping a fetish and of setting up
an idol, although they may appear the same, are really
very different, because when an idol is made it does not
always follow that it is worshiped. The word "idol"

comes from a Greek word meaning an *image* or *form*, and sometimes the idol is treated as only an image of the god or gods believed in, and is not mistaken for the god itself. Unhappily it has more frequently been regarded as a god, and believed to hear prayer, to accept gifts, and have power to bless or curse. The materials out of which different races shape their gods show us what their ideas are. These may be mere bundles of grass or rudely daubed stones, or carved with the care and beauty displayed in the household idols of the East. If the god is believed in as all-powerful, a huge image will be built, to which will be given a score of arms and legs, the head of a lion, the feet of a stag, and the wings of a bird. But it would fill a much larger book than this were I to tell you how in every age different nations have made and worshiped idols and what they have been like. Very many years will yet pass away before even in civilized countries people will learn that the great God has neither shape nor parts, and can never be looked upon, "seeing," as the good apostle Paul told the Greeks, "that He is Lord of heaven and earth, and dwelleth not in temples made with hands," and therefore is not "like unto gold or silver or stone graven by art and man's device."

XXVIII. NATURE-WORSHIP.

We have now to leave the lifeless things in which poor

savage man has found a god to hang round his neck or set up in his hut and learn a little about some of the living and moving things which are worshiped.

Some learned men think that the worship of serpents and trees was the earliest faith of mankind. Others have thought that the sun, moon, stars, and fire were first worshiped. But it seems more likely that in different parts of the world men had different gods, and would at first worship the things nearest to them till they knew enough about them to lessen fear, and would then bow before those greater powers whose mysteries are hidden still.

1. WATER-WORSHIP. The worship of water is very wide-spread and easy to account for—for what seemed so full of life, and therefore, according to early man's reason, so full of spirits, as rivers, brooks, and water-falls ? To him it was the water-demon that made the river flow so fast as to be dangerous in crossing, and that curled the dreaded whirlpool in which life was sucked. When one river-god came to be afterwards believed in, as controlling every stream, making it to flow lazily along or to rush at torrent-speed, it was believed to be wrong to save any drowning person lest the river-god should be cheated of his prey.

Sacred springs, holy wells, abound everywhere to show how deep and lasting was water-worship. You have heard of sacred rivers, such as the Ganges, of which some beautiful stories are given in the sacred books of India, telling how it flows from the heavenly places to bless the earth and wash away all sin.

2. TREE-WORSHIP. The worship of trees is also very common. The life that, locked up within them during the long winter, burst out in leaf and flower and fruit, and seemed to moan or whisper as the breezes shook branch and leaf, was that not also the sign of an indwelling spirit?

So, far later in time than the early nature-worshipers, the old Greeks thought when they peopled sea and stream, tree and hill, with beings whom they called nymphs, telling of the goddesses who dwelt in the water to bless the drinkers, and of those who were born and who died with the trees in which they lived. And you have perhaps heard that the priests of the ancient religion of this island held the oak-tree sacred and lived among its groves, as their name Druid, which comes from the Welsh word *derw* or the Greek *drus*, both meaning an *oak*, shows.

3. ANIMAL-WORSHIP. Besides the worship of trees and rivers and other like things seen to have life or motion, the worship of animals arose in very early times. The life in them was seen to be very different from that of the tree or river. The water swirled and foamed, the tree shook, the volcano hissed, but no eyes glistened from them, no huge claws sprang forth to tear. And the brute seemed so like to man in many things,

and withal was so much stronger, that it must have a soul greater than the soul of man.

As mastery over the brute was gained, the fear and worship of it died out here and there, but sacred animals play a great part in many religions. The kind of brute worshiped depended very much on the country in which man lived. In the far North he worshiped the bear and wolf, further South the lion and tiger and crocodile, and in very many parts of the world the serpent. So cunning and subtle seemed that long, writhing, brilliant-colored thing, so deadly was its poison-fang, so fascinating the glitter of the eye that looked out from its hateful face, that for long centuries it was feared and became linked in the minds of men as the soul of that Evil which early worked sorrow and shame among them.

On this I cannot now dwell, but must go on to tell you that man's next step, rising from the worship of stones and brutes, was to believe in a class of great gods each ruling some separate part of nature or of the life of men.

XXIX. POLYTHEISM, OR BELIEF IN MANY GODS.

Thus instead of thinking only of a separate spirit as dwelling in every streamlet, he conceived of one river-god or water-god ruling all streams, or of one sea-god ruling every sea. I hope you are taking notice of the lesson this history has so far taught, that the more man began to think and to know, the more did he lessen the number of his gods. Thus arose belief in one god ruling the thunder, another the rain, another the wind, another the sun, and so on.

As the best way of making quite clear to you the growth of belief in these great controlling beings, I will try and explain to you how the worship of the sun and moon began.

There is nothing that would excite man's wonder at first so much as the fact that daylight was not always with him, that for a time he could see things around him, and then that the darkness crept over them and caused him to grope along his path or lie down to rest.

Each morning, before the sun was seen, rays of light shot upward as if to herald his coming, and then he arrived to flood the earth with more light, growing brighter and brighter till the eye could scarce look upon him, so dazzling was the glory. Then as slowly he sank again, the light-rays lingering as they came until they passed away altogether.

About all the other gifts which the sun is made to shed upon this and other worlds you may read in books on astronomy (such as Mr. Lockyer's Lessons in that science), and from those you may learn true wonder-tales describing how we are all what the Incas of South America were called, "children of the sun;" here I am dealing with the sun as an object of worship only.

Welcome as was the light given by moon and far-off stars, it was less sure than the sun's, and, although it relieved the gloom and darkness, could not chase night away.

Therefore the natural feeling of man was to bow before this Lord of Light, and, in the earliest known form of adoration, kiss his hand to it, paying it the offering of sacrifice. There is an old story from some Jewish writings known as the Talmud, which describes very powerfully man's feeling concerning the darkness and the light.

It relates that when Adam and Eve were driven out of the garden of Eden, they wandered over the face of the earth. And the sun began to set, and they looked with fear at the lessening of the light, and felt a horror like death steal over their hearts. And the light of heaven grew paler and the wretched ones clasped one another in an agony of despair. Then all grew dark. And the luckless ones fell on the earth, silent, and thought that God had withdrawn from them the light for ever; and they spent the night in tears. But a beam of light began to rise over the eastern hills, after many hours of darkness, and the golden sun came back and dried the tears of Adam and Eve, and then they cried out with joy and said, "Heaviness may endure for a night, but joy cometh in the morning; this is a law that God hath laid upon nature."

The worship of the heavenly bodies is not only very wide-spread but continued to a late age among the great nations of the past, as the names of their gods and the remains of their temples prove. In this island pillars were once raised to the sun, and altars to the moon and the earth-goddess, while the story of early belief is preserved in the names given to some of the days of the week, as Sun-day, Mon- or Moon-day.

Days were the most ancient division of time, and as the changes of the moon began to be watched they marked the weeks, four weeks roughly making up the month which was seen to elapse between every new moon. To distinguish one day from another, names were given ; and as it was a belief that each of the seven planets presided over a portion of the day, their names were applied to the seven days of the week.

Our forefathers however consecrated the days of the week to their seven chief gods. Sunday and Monday to the sun and moon, as already stated ; Tuesday to *Tuisco* (which name, strange as it may seem, comes from the same word-root as *Deity*), father of gods and men ; Wednesday to *Woden* or *Odin*, one-eyed ruler of heaven and god of war ; Thursday to *Thor*, the god of thunder ; Friday to *Friga*, Woden's wife ; Saturday either to *Seater*, a Saxon god, or to *Saturn*. We use the name for each month of the year which the Romans gave, but the Saxon names were very different, January being called the *wolf-monat* or wolf-month, March the *lenet-monat*, because the days were seen to *lengthen*, and so on.

I should tell you that there are countries where, because the heat of the sun is so fierce as to scorch and wither plant and often cause death to man, he is not worshiped as the giver of the blessed light, but feared as an evil, malicious god.

The worship of fire is usually found joined to that of sun, moon and stars. Fire gives light and warmth ; it seems, in its wonderful power to lick up all that is heaped upon it, like some hungry, never-satisfied demon, and is nearest of anything on earth to the great fire bodies in the sky.

XXX. DUALISM, OR BELIEF IN TWO GODS.

Man, as he came to think more and more about things, and not to be simply frightened into an unreasoning worship of living and dead objects, lessened still further the number of ruling powers, and seemed to see two mighty gods fighting for mastery over himself and the universe.

On the one hand was a power that appeared to dwell in the calm, unclouded blue, and with kind and loving heart to scatter welcome gifts upon men; on the other hand was a power that appeared to be harsh and cruel, that lashed the sea into fury, covered earth and sky with blackness, swept man's home and crops away in torrent and in tempest, chilled him with icy hand, and gave his children to the beast of prey. One a god of light, smiling in the sunbeam ; the other a god of darkness, scowling in the thundercloud ; one ruling by good and gentle spirits, the other by fierce and evil spirits.

This belief in a good god opposed and fought against by a bad god became so deeply rooted that no religion is quite free from it, for it seemed to man the only explanation of the hurt and evil whose power he felt.

But it is not true that the Almighty God in whom we are taught to believe is checked and hindered by another power. If He were, He would cease to be all-mighty, and we should have to pray to the evil power and beseech *him* not to hurt us.

The sin which is in the world, and about which your own heart tells you, has its birth in the will of man, which God in His sovereign wisdom has created free. Instead of making us as mere machines that cannot go wrong, He has given us the awful power of doing either good or evil, and thus of showing our love to Him by choosing what He loves and doing the things that are pleasing in His sight. However anxious we may be, as man has so often been, to cast the blame of wrong-doing on another, the sins which we commit are our own willful work. This we know to be true because it is declared by that Voice within each of us which does not lie, and which is the voice of the holy God.

If we have power to break God's commandments, but not power to keep them, or if some unseen force, stronger than ourselves, is allowed to drive us into evil, we could not have that sense of guilt which ever follows sinning, because we should feel that the fault was not all our own, and that we should be wronged in being punished for what we could not help. Then that saddest of all states—distrust of God, distrust of His voice within—would be ours.

But leaving this matter for a while, I have hitherto said little about the way in which man would seek to express his feelings towards the gods in which he believed, be they few or many, good or bad. One way was by *praying* to them, another way by offering *sacrifice* to them.

XXXI. PRAYER.

To cry for help when we are in danger is our first act; to ask for what we want from those who seem able and willing to give it is both natural and right. Thus man prayed to his gods, and prays still, for to the end of time the deep long cry of mankind to Heaven will continue. And rude and hideous as may be the idol to which the poor savage tells his story of need or sorrow, we must, remember, stand in awe as we think of the soul within him that hungers for its food, even as the body hungers, and that yearns after the unseen God whom we call our Father in Heaven. Of course he prays in his ignorance for many weak and foolish things, to grant which would be really hurtful to him. In this he is like children who ask their parents for something which those parents know is not good for them, and who think themselves badly treated because they are denied it.

As man gets more thoughtful and trustful, he prays for better gifts than the things which perish, and, telling his wants and troubles to the All-wise Being, leaves it to Him to send whatever he may choose.

> " in His decision rest,
> Secure whate'er He gives, He gives the best."

XXXII. SACRIFICE.

The reason for offering sacrifices is explained by man's dealings with his fellow-man.

When we feel that we have vexed our friends, or that for some cause they are angry with us, our first desire is to remove the anger by an offering of some kind; while towards those whom we love and feel grateful for their kindness, we show our love and thanks by gifts.

In this way, sacrifices or offerings to idols, and to the seen and unseen powers of good and evil, began, and have continued in different forms among all nations to the present day; one sacrifice being offered from a feeling of thanksgiving, another as a bribe to quiet or appease the gods thought to be angry, and who, being looked upon very often as big men, were supposed to be humored like cross and sulky people.

Of course men would offer the best of what they had, and would pick the finest fruits and flowers as gifts to the

gods, or burn upon a raised pile of stones called an altar
the most spotless of their flocks. And because the sur-
render of the nearest and dearest was often thought necessary to allay the anger, or secure the help, or ward off
the vengeance of the god, the lives of the dear ones were
offered, and this is one of the chief causes of the hideous
and horrid rites which curdle one's blood to think about,
and of which every land and every age have been the
spectators.

The blessed Father of all "is not a God of the dead,
but of the living," and a Being who therefore loves not
the sacrifice of blood and death. The sacrifice which is
sweet to Him is that of hearts which, sorrowful for their
sins and for grieving Him by wandering from His father-
ly arms, are willing to give up their wrong-doings, and,
casting out selfishness, in which so much evil lurks, to do
His will on earth as it is done in heaven. Men are only
now slowly learning this great truth, although many centuries have passed away since it was first taught, because
they have found it easier to profess certain beliefs or pay
others to perform certain rites for them, than to strive
day by day to obey the commandments of God.

XXXIII. MONOTHEISM, OR BELIEF IN ONE GOD.

Coming much nearer the time when the history of
man's religious belief grows clearer, we see that his
ideas had become higher and nobler.

It had at first seemed to him as if in heaven above and earth beneath naught but confusion reigned, but as the course of things became more carefully watched, it was seen that order, not disorder; plan, not blind fate, ruled the universe.

The storm which made havoc with the fruit of man's industry swept disease and foul air away; the fire that, uncontrolled, destroyed, was, when controlled, man's useful servant; the night that filled the air with bad spirits, lulled man to welcome rest; the things which had been looked upon as curses, turned out to be blessings, and much that seemed discord in nature was harmony to him who touched the chords aright.

Man had at first worshiped that which was *strongest*, and feared that which seemed likeliest to harm him most; but as he grew in knowledge and wisdom, he came to worship that which was *best*. This arose from the feeling, which I have just described, that something else than crushing force was over all. We have seen that on man's first entrance into life he found it one continued battle against forces of all kinds, and the only law that ruled was the law of might. He who could get a thing and keep it was entitled to it. Besides ability to defend himself by sheer force or cunning, man possessed the power of injuring and of doing wanton cruelty and mischief for its own sake, and of this power all history shows us he made sad use. Lower in this than the beast which slays to satisfy its hunger, man killed his fellow-man to satisfy his lawless ambition, and committed ravages which centuries of labor have been unable to repair. But as the human family increased, it became clear that there would soon be an end to everything, did man continue using to the full this power to hurt, and plunder, and kill. Therefore to enable mankind to live together in peace and to progress, it was needful for them to feel that respect was due to the rights of others, and that it was necessary to do to them as they would wish to be done unto. If a man refused to agree to this, and in malice injured another, he was punished for breaking the rules which must be kept to make what is called *society* possible. But besides the sense of duty towards others, there was another and a deeper sense by which man felt that it was wrong to injure them.

There is something within everyone, when called upon to choose between a better and a worse, which speaks in clear and certain tones.

If we are tempted to do wrong, yet know to do right, from whence comes the knowledge? If after each act of kindness, each duty faithfully done, there follows a blessed peace, from whence does it spring? Sun and moon cannot be spoken of as knowing right from wrong, or as helping us to discern the difference. The stars of heaven and the stones of earth know nothing about duties, and are moved or kept still by other laws than the law of love.

God is its source, and none other but He.

" His that gentle voice we hear,
  Soft as the breath of even,
That checks each fault, that calms each fear,
  And speaks forgiven."

Never, I beseech you, stifle Conscience, for when
it speaks you are in the path of danger; only when you
are safe is it silent, yet none the less watchful, unsleep-
ing. Never, I beseech you, try to displace that judge
who never leaves his seat, but sits moment by moment
weighing every thought and act in his balance.

For that which we feel and know to be the highest
law within us must, we rightly argue, dwell in perfection
in Him whose authority thus makes itself heard by us.
And since God's laws are the creatures of His love, it
follows that to obey them is to dwell in love, and therefore to dwell in God.

So man, footsore and toilworn, came at last to rest in
this, and to believe in One God and Father of all,
"maker of heaven and earth, and of all things visible
and invisible," and to believe that " to love Him with all
the heart is more than all whole burnt-offerings and
sacrifices."

In some such way as I have tried to show you did
man arrive at this sublimest of all beliefs. But only a
few out of the large human family are thus blessed; the
greater number still worship gods many, gods good, bad,
and indifferent.

Even where a belief in one God has been reached,
He has at first been shaped in the mind after the fashion

of a man. To the people dwelling in the cold, bleak North, he was the Thunderer ; to the people dwelling further South on the coast that bordered quiet waters and under sunny skies, he was the Beautiful; to the dweller in the plain, strong in soul and rough in dealing, he was a power walking on the wings of the wind, a being with the feelings and passions of a man.

It needed great teachers who walked amidst the groves of beautiful Athens, and a greater still who sat wearied by a well in Samaria, to convey ideas of God which cannot be surpassed.

And yet history tells us that in this as in other things nations have fallen back. They have forgotten God as the children of Israel did when, after receiving His commandment to worship no graven imagine, they shaped an idol like the sacred bull of the Egypt they had left.

Just as there are savage races still in that Stone Age, which, I have shown you, was the beginning of progress, and which Europe has left thousands of years behind, so there are to be found races that have not risen above the lowest ideas about spirits in lifeless things. *They show us what we were ; we represent what, it is hoped, they may become.* In believing this we gain trust that, since God has made nothing in vain, He will give to the poor and wild and ignorant to know in the hereafter, what, through no fault of theirs, has been hidden from them here,

XXXIV. THREE STORIES ABOUT ABRAHAM.

Since the highest belief of any time is the belief of its highest minds, it is clear that in every age there have been men more far-seeing and thoughtful than their fellow-men, who, feeling that this great, solemn life is given for something nobler than eating and money-getting, asked themselves why they were at all; whither they were going; and from whence came what they saw around them. Of the holy lives with which such men enriched the earth, and of the wise and beautiful thoughts in which they have recorded their search after truth, which is but another name for search after God, you will learn by and by; but I want to redeem my promise and tell you a little about one of these men, earliest in historic time, who is thought to have laid hold of and given to us through others a belief in the One God.

Abraham, for he it is whom I mean, was a native of the country called Chaldea. The clear sky of that Eastern land invited the people dwelling in it to the charmful study of the sun, moon, and stars, and they not only worshiped these bodies, but sought to foretell the fate of men from them. An ancient historian tells us that every Chaldean had a signet and staff bearing the sign of the planet or stars that were seen at his birth. Some have said that Ur, the city where Abraham was born, was a chief seat of sun-worship, and that its name means light or fire. We may safely say that Abraham's early years were spent among sun-worshipers, and it may interest you to know that his name and memory are held in high honor, not only by the Jews, but also by the Persians and Mohammedans.

Among the stories about him which are preserved in certain ancient books are the following.

Terah, the father of Abraham, was a maker and dealer in idols. Being obliged to go from home one day, he left Abraham in charge. An old man came in and asked the price of one of the idols. " Old man," said Abraham, "how old art thou ?" " Threescore years," answered the old man. " Threescore years!" said Abraham, " and thou wouldst worship a thing that my father's slaves made in a few hours ? Strange that a man of sixty should bow his gray head to a creature such as that." The man, crimsoned with shame, turned away ; and then came a grave-looking woman to bring an offering to the gods. " Give it them thyself," said Abraham ; " thou wilt see how greedily they will eat it." She did so. Abraham then took a hammer and broke all the idols except the largest, in whose hands he placed the hammer. When Terah returned, he asked angrily what profane wretch had dared thus to abuse the gods. " Why," said Abraham, " during thine absence a woman brought yonder food to the gods and the younger ones began to eat. The old god, enraged at their boldness, took the hammer and smashed them." " Dost thou mock thy aged father ?" said Terah ; "do I not know that they can neither

eat nor move ?"   " And yet," said Abraham, " thou wor-
shipest them, and wouldst have me worship them too."
The story adds that Terah, in his rage, sent Abraham to
be judged for his crime by the king.

Nimrod asked Abraham : You will not adore the idols
of your father.   Then pray to fire.

Abraham : Why may I not pray to water, which will
quench fire ?

Nimrod : Be it so : pray to water.

Abraham : But why not to the clouds which hold the
water ?

Nimrod : Well, then, pray to the clouds.

Abraham : Why not to the wind, which drives the
clouds before it ?

Nimrod : Then pray to the wind.

Abraham : Be not angry, O King—I cannot pray to
the fire or the water or the clouds or the wind, but to
the Creator who made them : Him only will I worship.

On another occasion, " Abraham left a cave in which
he had dwelt and stood on the face of the desert.   And
when he saw the sun shining in all its glory, he was
filled with wonder ; and he thought, ' Surely the sun is
God the Creator,' and he knelt down and worshiped the
sun.   But when evening came, the sun went down in
the west, and Abraham said, ' No, the Author of creation cannot set.'   Now the moon arose in the east, and
the stars looked out of the sky.   Then said Abraham,
' This moon must indeed be God, and all the stars are

His host.' And kneeling down he adored the moon. But the moon set also, and from the east appeared once more the sun's bright face. Then said Abraham, 'Verily these heavenly bodies are no gods, for they obey law ; I will worship Him whose laws they obey.' "

XXXV. MAN'S BELIEF IN A FUTURE LIFE.

The rude beliefs about spirits and dreams and the customs observed at burials show us that, however shapeless man's idea of another life may be, he has from the earliest times believed that the spirit or *breath*, the ghost (which comes from the same root as *gust*), departs to dwell elsewhere when the body is cold and still in death. The highest and lowest races of men have tried to form some notion of what that blessed state is like where happiness is given to the good, where friends " loved long since and lost awhile," will, with smiling angel-faces, welcome us ; or what that dark state may be where misery and wanhope (despair) dwell.

Man, in wondering what becomes of the spirit, has thought that it haunted the place where it once lived, or that it passed into some other body, perhaps into some animal, and then into higher and higher forms, until it reached the dwelling-place of the gods.

He has placed his heaven in some far-off Island of the Blest, or in some sunny land,

> " Deep meadow'd, happy, fair with orchard lawns,
> And bowery hollows crown'd with summer sea,"

or in the west where the sun sets, or in the sun, moon,
and stars themselves.   The pictures of it have been
copied from the earth ; and all that he loves here, whether
chaste or coarse, he hopes to have in larger measure
there, even as he wishes to shut out from thence all that
he dreads now.

The best and brightest view of heaven is, leaving the
rude idea of the savage far behind, to behold in every
place on earth a fit spot whereon to kneel, to feel the
sacredness of duty, and then we shall believe that all
which we here know to be highest and noblest and best
shall be ours in heaven, wherever that heaven may be.
The thought that God's worlds are thus linked together
is very beautifully touched upon in one of the old Per-
sian sacred books.   The soul of a good man is pictured
as being met in the other world by a lovely maiden,
"noble, with brilliant face, one of fifteen years, as fair in
her growth as the fairest creatures.   Then to her speaks
the soul of the pure man, asking, ' What maiden art thou
whom I have seen here as the fairest of maidens in body ?'
She answers, ' I am, O youth, thy good thoughts, words,
and works, thy good law, the own law of thine own
body.   Thou hast made the pleasant yet pleasanter to
me, the fair yet fairer.' "*

And since all of us like to read hymns about heaven,

* The whole of this beautiful story is given by Mr. Tylor in his " Primitive Culture," vol. ii. p. 90, a work to which I am much indebted, and
which should receive careful attention from every thoughtful person.

here is one which I expect you have never seen before. It was written thousands of years ago by some great-souled Aryan, and is full of music that cannot die away:

Where there is eternal light, in the world where the sun is placed, in that immortal, imperishable world, place me, O Soma!

Where king Vaivasvata reigns, where the secret place of heaven is, where these mighty waters are, there make me immortal!

Where life is free, in the third heaven of heavens, where the worlds are radiant, there make me immortal !

Where wishes and desires are, where the place of the bright sun is, where there is freedom and delight, there make me immortal !

Where there is happiness and delight, where joy and pleasure reside, where the desires of our desire are attained, there make me immortal !

XXXVI. SACRED BOOKS.

If this book has taught you nothing else, I hope it has taught you that the different beliefs of mankind about God are worthy of attention.

Few of us will live here for more than sixty or seventy years; and when we take off the time needed for eating and working and sleeping, there is not so very much left wherein to learn a little about the world in which we are sent to dwell. We do wisely to use some spare moments in asking how other eyes have looked upon the beauty and the mystery around, and what it has said to their hearts.

It is not so very long ago that good-meaning men looked upon the various religions of the world as almost beneath notice, or if studied at all, studied as proofs of man's hatred to the good and the true. But wiser and more thoughtful men felt that we ought to try and understand them, and see what kind of answers others have given to the questions about God, and the wide universe, and life and death, which we all ask. These answers may be feeble and dim, but since they are the best that could be had, they demand our respect. We do not make our own religion more true by calling other religions false, nor do we make it worth less to us by admitting the good that may be in them. And the lesson which even a slight knowledge of the sacred books of other faiths, some older than our own, and still believed in by hundreds of millions of mankind, teaches, is that God has never been without a witness among them. These sacred books, which they look upon as His word to them, are as dear to them as our Bible is dear to us. In them are the precepts which they have been taught to obey, the prayers and hymns which have the full rich meaning age alone can give, and which no new words could bring. It is true that these books contain many silly stories, myths, legends, coarse ideas about God ; but from these no ancient book is free, and the errors that they contain do not make less true whatever of truth they hold. A diamond is not less a diamond because we pick it out of a dust heap.

Any account which I might give you of the different sacred writings would be chiefly a list of very long names, and it is better that I should prove the truth of what has been said by quoting some hymns and prayers from them.

The hymn about heaven comes from the very old sacred book of the Brahmans; here is part of another hymn from the same:

In the beginning there arose the source of golden light.

He was the only born Lord of all that is.

He stablished the earth and this sky; who is the God to whom we shall offer our sacrifice?

He who gives life, He who gives strength; whose blessing all the bright gods desire; whose shadow is immortality; whose shadow is death.

Who is the God to whom we shall offer sacrifice?

He who through His power is the only King of the breathing and awakening world; He whose power these snowy mountains and the sea and distant river proclaim.

He through whom the heaven was established—nay, the highest heaven; He who measured out the light in the air.

This hymn-prayer is from the same book. Varuná, the god addressed, was one of their chief gods, and means the "Surrounder:"

Let me not yet, O Varuna, enter into the house of clay. Have mercy, Almighty, have mercy!

Through want of strength, have I done wrong: Have mercy, Almighty, have mercy!

Whenever we men, O Varuna, commit an offense before the heavenly host, whenever we break the law through thoughtlessness, have mercy, Almighty, have mercy!

Here are some precepts from one of the sacred books of the Buddhists, which would find a fit place in our own beautiful Book of Proverbs:

Conquer anger by mildness, evil by good, falsehood by truth.

Be not desirous of discovering the faults of others, but zealously guard against your own.

He is a more noble warrior who subdues himself, than he who in battle conquers thousands. (Compare with this Proverbs xvi. 32.)

To the virtuous all is pure. Therefore think not that going unclothed, fasting, or lying on the ground, can make the impure pure, for the mind will still remain the same.

I believe that Jesus Christ would say to every Brahman and Buddhist who strove to obey these precepts, the words which fell cheeringly upon the Jewish lawyer's ear, " Thou art not far from the kingdom of God."

XXXVII. CONCLUSION.

Histories are often so made up of dates, giving the years when kings began to reign, when they died, and when famous battles were fought, that I dare say this early history of man, which has scarcely a date in it, seems a rather vague and confused story.

But we have been traveling through ages so vast, that I might have confused you still more if I had spoken of years the number of which none of us can grasp, and put down guess-work figures with long rows of ciphers after them.

It is through that twilight time of which I told you in the first pages of this little book that I have sought to take you. I have guessed as little as possible, and brought common sense to interpret the story which bones, flint knives, metal weapons, picture-writings, words, and other things contain, seeing in it a tale of progress, slow but sure, which began at the beginning of time, and will go on until time shall cease to be.

I wish I could have made that story appear as beautiful and fascinating to you as it is to myself, but I thought it better told even roughly than not told at all.

The facts of science are not, as some think, dry, lifeless things. They are living things, filling with sweetest poetry the ear that listens to them, and with fadeless harmony of colors the eye that looks upon them.

They not only give us these higher pleasures which endure, but they bring daily bread and health and comfort to thousands, who but for knowledge of them would have lived pitiful lives.

I am offering you good counsel in advising you to use a certain portion of your time in studying one branch of science. It matters not which you choose so far as wonder, beauty and truth are concerned, for astronomy, botany, chemistry, geology, alike possess these in such abundance that life will be too short to exhaust them.

With the mind thus stored, many an hour, otherwise dull, will be "filled with music;" many a star-lit night, otherwise unheeded, will shine with familiar lights; many a landscape, bald and ugly to the unseeing eye, marked with lines of beauty traced by its Maker's hand. And if God, as I think this story shows, has chosen that man's progress shall largely depend upon himself, how careful should we be to do nothing that will be a hindrance. Our knowledge is no blessing to us, unless we have learned to use it well and wisely, and learned too that with it only, life is not complete. If, dealing with the " things we see," it walk hand in hand with faith in the unseen, these two shall make life beautiful and blessed.

GOD GIVES THEE YOUTH BUT ONCE. KEEP THOU
   THE CHILDLIKE HEART THAT WILL HIS KINGDOM BE;
THE SOUL PURE-EYED THAT, WISDOM-LED, E'EN NOW
   HIS BLESSED FACE SHALL SEE.

THE END.

HALF HOUR
Recreations in Popular Science

25 cents per Part; $2.50 for twelve consecutive Parts.

No. 1. *Strange Discoveries respecting the Aurora and recent Solar Researches.* By Richard A. Proctor, F.R.A.S.

No 2. *The Cranial Affinities of Man and the Ape.* By Prof. Rudolph Virchow, of Berlin, author of "Cellular Pathology." Fully Illustrated.

No. 3. *Spectrum Analysis Explained,* and its Uses to Science Illustrated. With a Colored Plate and several Wood Cuts.

No. 4. *Spectrum Analysis Discoveries,* showing its Application in Microscopical Research and to Discoveries of the Physical Constitution and Movements of the Heavenly Bodies. From the works of Schellen, Young, Roscoe, Lockyer, Huggins and others.

No. 5. *Nebulæ, Meteoric Showers and Comets.*

No. 6. *Unconscious Action of the Brain, and Epidemic Delusions.* By Dr. Carpenter, author of "The Microscope and its Revelations," "Human Physiology," &c.

No. 7. *The Geology of the Stars.* By Prof. A. Winchell, of the University of Michigan, author of "Sketches of Creation."

The Unity of Natural Phenomena.

An Introduction to the Study of

THE FORCES OF NATURE.

Being a popular explanation of the latest discoveries in the domain of Natural Science, including the "Correlation of Forces," Mode of Motion," "Force of Gravity," and Mutual Convertibility of the Forces of Nature." From the French of EMILE SAIGEY, with notes and an introduction by PROF. T. F. MOSES, of Urbana University.

1 volume, crown 8vo. $1.50.

"In this charming treatise, M. Emile Saigey gives a very lucid account of the latest mode of speculating on the Physical Facts of the Universe. It is a mode which may be described as bringing *all the resources of modern science* to the proof of the fact that the human mind is incapable of any intelligible conception of physical facts which does not resolve itself into matter and motion. There is in fact but *one science* under many names, and that science is mechanics. Atoms, and the laws which regulate their movements,—this is all our material universe."—*Blackwood's Magazine.*

Any of the above sent free by mail on receipt of price.

HIGHER LAW. A Romance. By the author of "The Pilgrim and the Shrine." 12mo, cloth. $1.75

"There is no novel, in short, which can be compared to it for its width of view, its cultivation, its poetry, and its deep human interest, * * except 'Romola.'" —*Westminster Review.*

"Its careful study of character, and the ingenuity and independence of its speculations, will commend it to the admiration even of those who differ from its conclusions most gravely." —*British Quarterly Review.*

THE PILGRIM AND THE SHRINE. Third Edition. 12mo. cloth. - - $1.50

"One of the wisest and most charming of books."
— *Westminster Review.*

BY-AND-BY, by the same author. $1.75

EXETER HALL.—A Theological Romance. "One of the most exciting romances of the day."
Paper, 60 cents. Cloth, .80

HALF-HOURS with Modern Scientists. Containing valuable Lectures and Essays by Wallace, Roscoe, Huggins, Lockyer, Young, Mayer and Rood.
$2.00

LECTURES ON INSTINCT. By P. A. Chadbourne, A.M., M.D., late President University of Wisconsin, author of "Natural Theology," "The Relations of Natural History," Etc. 1 vol. 12mo. $1.75

LEAVES FROM THE BOOK OF NATURE. By M. Schele de Vere. New edition, with Vignettes, $1.50

WONDERS OF THE DEEP. By M. Schele de Vere. Fourth Edition, Illustrated, $1.50 ; full gilt, - - - - - $2.00

"One of the freshest, most scientific, and at the same time most popular and delightful books of the kind we have ever read."
—*St. John's Telegraph.*

Any of the above sent free by mail on receipt of price.

HALF-HOURS WITH THE MICROSCOPE.

By EDWIN LANKESTER, M.D., F.R.S. Illustrated by 250 Drawings from Nature. 18mo. cloth, $1.00.

"This beautiful little volume is a very complete manual for the amateur microscopist. * * The 'Half-Hours' are filled with clear and agreeable descriptions, whilst eight plates, executed with the most beautiful minuteness and sharpness, exhibit no less than 250 objects with the utmost attainable distinctness."—*Critic*.

HALF-HOURS WITH THE TELESCOPE:

Being a popular Guide to the Use of the Telescope as a means of Amusement and Instruction. Adapted to inexpensive Instruments. By R. A. PROCTOR, B. A., F. R. A. S. 18mo, cloth, with Illustrations on stone and wood. Price, $1.00.

"It is crammed with starry plates on wood and stone, and among the celestial phenomena described or figured, by far the larger number may be profitably examined with small telescopes."—*Illustrated Times*.

HALF-HOURS WITH THE STARS:

A Plain and Easy Guide to the Knowledge of the Constellations; showing in twelve Maps, the Position of the Principal Star-Groups Night after Night throughout the Year, with introduction and a separate explanation of each Map. True for every Year. By RICHARD A. PROCTOR, B. A., F. R. A. S. Demy 4to. Price, $2.25.

"Nothing so well calculated to give a rapid and thorough knowledge of the position of the stars in the firmament has ever been designed or published hitherto. Mr. Proctor's "Half-Hours with the Stars" will become a text-book in all schools, and an invaluable aid to all teachers of the young."—*Weekly Times*.

MANUAL OF POPULAR PHYSIOLOGY:

Being an Attempt to Explain the Science of Life in Untechnical Language. By HENRY LAWSON, M. D. 18mo, with 90 Illustrations. Price, $1.00.

Man's Mechanism, Life, Force, Food, Digestion, Respiration, Heat, the Skin, the Kidneys, Nervous System, Organs of Sense, &c., &c., &c.

"Dr. Lawson has succeeded in rendering his manual amusing as well as instructive. All the great facts in human physiology are presented to the reader successively; and either for private reading or for classes, this manual will be found well adapted for initiating the uninformed into the mysteries of the structure and functions of their own bodies."—*Athenæum*.

A DICTIONARY OF DERIVATIONS

Of the English Language, in which each word is traced to its primary root. Forming a Text-Book of Etymology, with Definitions and the Pronunciation of each word. 16mo. $1.00.

A HAND BOOK OF SYNONYMS

Of the English Language, with Definitions, &c, 16mo, cloth. $1.00.

₊ These two Manuals are very comprehensive in a small compass.

Any of the above sent free by mail on receipt of price.

www.ingramcontent.com/pod-product-compliance
Lightning Source LLC
Chambersburg PA
CBHW020034030726
47499CB00007B/2418